A BUMPY RIDE

By
Essie Thomas

Jo: Gary
5/8/09

[signature] Essie Thomas

TEACH Services, Inc.
Brushton, New York

2009 10 11 12 13 14 · 5 4 3 2 1

Published by

TEACH Services, Inc.
www.TEACHServices.com

If you get to it,
God will get you through it

INTRODUCTION

As I write this book, I believe and trust that it will be a source of encouragement to everyone who reads it. I especially hope that my story will inspire those who are struggling with adversity to persevere and remain hopeful as they seek the light. When I was going through an ugly divorce, as my son was being punished unjustly for thirteen years, and as my father was passing away, friends and family would ask me; "How do you cope and maintain your sanity?" Of course I would get upset and feel the same pressure as anyone else; but I knew that I must try to maintain my composure, so that I could work through my problems, and interact with those around me, especially those directly involved in that particular situation.

At one time or another, each of us is faced with some type of dilemma. Even during the worst times and most unpleasant situations, you come to realize that there are millions of people who are faced daily with more difficult conditions and circumstances. By comparing your situation with those less fortunate, you can gain some encouragement and courage and become better able to move forward and seek solutions to problems. Sometimes multiple situations happen at once, but you must gather up enough courage and determination, with the help of God, to get you through whatever faces you.

My friends and family encouraged me to write this book, as they insisted that it would be a great help to others, after they saw the way that I struggled to keep composure while dealing with some heartbreaking dilemmas. I hope that this book will inspire each reader and give confidence, hope and in the belief that bad times do not last forever. Cultivate determination to work hard, and always do your best. God has given everyone some kind of talent or gift, and He will never leave you. You must never lose sight of the basic truth: even when life's road is bumpy and hard, embrace the challenge and know that God will get you through it.

CONTENTS

CHAPTER ONE

CHALLENGES, HOW AND WHY

Some of the most important of life's lessons are learned through some of the hardest times. No matter how hard these situations are, you eventually will move past them. It may take minutes, hours, days, or even years to resolve; but eventually even the hardest times become distant memories. Often times one may feel that no matter how much courage one can muster, there is no end in sight. Reflect on some of life's experiences, as I do and remind yourself of the power of your beliefs and your determination to learn through life's previous lessons, and/or perhaps your belief in God. You continue to hold on to what allows you to work through the situation, and prepare for that bumpy ride. As you focus and begin to reflect on your life, you start analyzing various times and events that were challenging, and you wonder: *How did I ever manage to get through this situation?* Yet, somehow you do, because if you get to it, God will get you through it.

At this stage in my life, I can look back and evaluate the amazing challenges during the last few decades. As events unfolded I began to question, "What did I do wrong to deserve this? Why me?" I then asked God to grant me the strength to pass the test, if He indeed was testing me. During some of the darkest times in my life, it seemed that everyone else around me was doing just fine, or at least not being faced with the type of problems or situations that I was experiencing.

Someone once said, "Don't judge a book by the cover" and "You are just on the outside looking in." I found these statements to be very true as I talked and listened to others. Each person and each family has faced some challenges in their life at one point or another. While one person may be facing a particular heartache, another is facing a very different one. You may be struggling with health, finance, relationship, legal matters, or family matters, and trying to use all the courage and strength that you can generate to meet your challenge and move on. Life is a series of problems. You are either facing one at present, have just gone through one; or perhaps you are getting ready to go through another different period. Sometimes it seems that no matter what you try or think the solution might be, it seems not to work. Yet, you must stay focused and try something else until you do succeed. Even after all this, you know you are still in for a bumpy ride. Once you discover some of the problems and situations that others are experiencing, you may be surprised that you would keep your problem instead of trading for what others are facing. Another person's challenge may be much worse than yours. Life teaches us that no matter how bad things are in our lives, there is always something good for which we can thank God. Even when situations improve, we must remember that there are still things we need to work on in our lives. You learn to focus on your purpose and not your problems, because when you start to focus completely on the problems, you become consumed by the problems, which then lead to self-centeredness. Everything turns into a state of "my problems, my issues, my pains," or in other words, my pity party. You must let go of this inward focus and direct your focus toward God and to helping those around you. The greatest gift happens when you begin to share love and reach out to touch and help others. By focusing on others, you learn to deal with both the good and the bad things in life.

After you refocus your energy, you may realize that there is a solution to your problems, and those persons or situations that you thought were doing great, are not so great after all. You realize that your problem is not as overwhelming as you originally thought, and you feel empowered to deal with your situation. For example, if you have been blessed with good health, you are already ahead of millions of people and have much more energy and focus to direct toward your goals. If you wake up in the morning and have more health than illness, you are blessed. If you are not feeling the agony of torture or the pangs of starvation; if you have food to eat, clothes on your back, a roof over your head and a place to sleep, you are richer than almost 80% of the people in the world. You are blessed. If you can attend church or any other meeting without the fear of being harassed, tortured, arrested or even put to death, you are blessed beyond over half the world's population. If you have not felt the loneliness of prison, you are blessed over millions of people. If you have money in the bank, wallet or purse, you are among the top seven to eight percent of the world's wealthy people. If you are reading this book, you are among those who not only are able to read, but are able to choose what they read. Hopefully you now realize just how blessed you truly are, and you should feel grateful to have your current difficulty, and not some more devastating crisis. If you want to feel really rich, just start counting all the things that you have that money cannot buy. Start living, and stop worrying. Realize just how blessed you really are. Take a deep breath, focus on how you are blessed beyond millions of other people and ask yourself, *"What can I learn from this experience and how can I move on?"* In your happiest moment, praise God; when difficulties arise, seek God's help; when you have quiet moments, worship God. Never forget to trust God and thank Him for every moment of your life.

All of these thoughts and more came to my mind as I was dealing with some challenges in my life that needed attention. I was in desperate need for God's grace as I tried to resolve an ugly divorce that dragged on for more than five years. During this time, I drained myself mentally, physically and financially to get justice for our only child, Keagan, as he was incarcerated unjustly. I constantly tried to remind myself that these trials would soon pass, and there is a reason for everything. This brick wall that has been placed in front of us has a purpose. Although we may never know what God has in store for us, we can believe that there is a reason for every situation in life.

You may find yourself depressed, annoyed, or angry, and you may break down and just cry at times. I knew that my anger was unhealthy, and had to turn those angry feelings into positive energy. I tried to come up with a strategy that would help resolve or help my situations. Anger will only interfere with your freedom, and affect how you love and act toward others. Anger will create a barrier to life and others. Always try to resolve the anger with whatever or whoever is involved, and leave that emotion from the anger behind.

Reach for courage, and say positive and encouraging things to your love ones; try to keep their spirits up with a positive attitude. Hide your negative feelings and display the situation in a positive light. If you feel that there is no way past your problem, take a moment to pray as I did, and still do. Prayer is the most powerful channel of communication; you will be surprised and amazed at how much it will help you make a decision.

CHAPTER TWO

STRUGGLES, VALUES, INTEGRITY AND ENDURANCE

Struggles and challenges have not been strangers in my life, as many of my friends and family can attest. I have drawn strength, determination and perseverance from my family life and religious beliefs. A loving family support has always been a part of my life. I grew up with my mother, Jane, my father Jessie, and four sisters, Shirley, Jewel, Alice, and Dorothy, and two brothers Jessie and Johnny. We lived in a small southern town in Alabama, where family and community were most prevalent in every phase of our lives. Having a loving atmosphere in your home is very important. The most powerful force in life is love, and it can help overcome many difficulties. The whole community: grandparents, uncles, aunts, cousins and friends were all concerned and involved with each person's well being. No matter where I was, I was constantly aware of my behavior, for almost any adult in the neighborhood would help with disciplining the children, as well as reporting behavior back to the parents for additional discipline. We thrived in this community, because their love was much greater than their threats.

It has been said, "It takes a whole village to raise a child." The neighborhood's concern and involvement required respect and manners that instilled morals and values into the core of each person's life. There is a lot to be said for a caring family in every culture and lifestyle. Even if the whole neighborhood isn't involved in a child's life, both the parents must be involved. Just as it takes two people to produce a child, two parent should be involved in the child's life. The lack of parental involvement has been proven to be the source of many of the social dysfunctions and outrageous behavior exhibited by some of the young people today.

Boys especially long for direction, love and leadership, but too often their role models come from the wrong type of characters. These bad character traits are learned and passed down, resulting in violent and direr consequences. Both parents must be involved in their children's lives in a positive way, especially the father. Each parent should be involved in a child's educational development. Obviously if the father has died, or is not part of the family due to some unfortunate circumstances, then allowances can be made. Fathers need to step up and become more involved in their children's lives, rather than merely producing offspring. Women also need to be more responsible, as mere children are becoming pregnant on a daily basis. Parents have to get back to being parents. They must concentrate more on their parental duties than trying to gain their children's friendship. Parents should monitor their children's friends, and know who they are communicating with on the computer, MySpace or any other space.

Parents must get involved in their children's lives before the children become involved with something terrible that demands the parent's attention. Disagreements and discussions between family members are normal, but you should strive to mend broken relationships with family members when they occur. Sincere efforts must be made to establish a civil relationship with any family member when the relationship and communication have been cut off. It is great to have the support of friends, but, nothing can compare to a caring and supportive family.

I know from experience the positive aspects of the support of a strong family network. I have had discussions with many people who have lost contact and communication with various family members for different reasons. If these people made the effort to re-establish contact with their family members, and gain these relationships back, they would be much happier and more content. Their lives would be more peaceful, and more of their energies could be directed to other things. It is not always what we have in our lives, but who we have in our lives.

As I have observed the young people of today, and their lack of morals, and respect for themselves and others, I crave for the caring and discipline from my childhood community that helped guide and shape productive lives. It appears that most of the focus to-day is towards material things, and this has become the measurement by which much of society is mea-sured and judged. We have become consumed with obtaining material things by whatever means possi-ble to impress our friends and family. This obsession make us lose sight of what should be the real value and focus of life. We must never lose sight of the ba-sics for a balanced life, the encouragement of pride, morals and respect for oneself, especially where chil-dren are involved. Without some basic structure, car-ing, concern, discipline and love, one does not have these morals and values to reflect back on when chal-lenges are presented and a rational decision has to be made. Without the basic structure is a recipe for failure.

One might fail to realize that certain behavior contributes to delinquency. Parents cultivate delinquency from infancy when they give their children everything that they want. These children grow up believing that the world will give them whatever they desire. When these children start to pick up foul words, many parents laugh, showing them a form of approval and making them believe that this is cute. They are thus encouraged to pick up even more of those "cute" words and phrases. When a parent does everything for their children, picking up their toys, books, and clothing, this also gives the wrong message. These children learn to pass all their responsibility to others. It is no wonder that many children are the way they are today. We need to take a good look at what contributed to their behavior.

Modern life is constantly changing. Developing technology has played a tremendous part in most people's lives. We have come a long way from a typewriter to computers, from vinyl records to CDs and DVDs; so many things have advanced and changed. Yet, unique values such as integrity, loyalty, respect, and honestly have been and still are, what will distinguish us as good human beings. Integrity is our most prized possession. We must not compromise our values. We may have multiplied our possessions, but we have reduced our values and become more concerned with attraction by appearance than by substance.

Popular diversions come along that present what seems to be an easy life. Involvement in drugs, prostitution, gangs or anything that appears to get the person some attention, notice or respect seems to attract our young people. One should never become so enthralled with such things that they will do anything, denying values and integrity, to fit in. We must be willing to teach self-respect and real values to our children. They should be taught to ask themselves, "Am I being guided and driven by pressure? Am I being driven by bitterness? Am I being driven by guilt? Am I being driven by materialism for possessions to gain popularity? Am I being selfish to try to achieve this at the expense of others?" Selfishness will not allow people to work together, their egos get in the way. When we promote the ego and let the ego take over, we are allowing ourselves to lose many loving and caring relationships in our lives.

Throughout this type of life this person will miss out on the respect, caring and love of others. These people wonder why others do not want to befriend or associate with them. It is time that we stop worrying and spending lot of energy on superficial things to impress others, but instead look inside ourselves to understand what really matters in our lives. It is time for this isolation to cease, and focus on becoming part of a more positive environment.

Parents and guardians must be instructive and willing to guide their children. Examine yourself if necessary, and see what it is that alienates others, and then take immediate steps to correct these character flaws. We must teach our children to concentrate on God's purpose for their lives. God is much more interested in who we are than what we do. We are called human beings, not human doings. Each person has a choice which has a consequence; they should not be affected by any fads or temptations of which they are confronted.

Sometimes it is better to be alone than in the wrong company. Self-reliance and independence is one of the greatest accomplishments. A person should be wary of those who quickly want to become friends for a seemingly minor reason. One must keep their eyes open for the catch. Do you think someone would offer you something by stating all the devastation, ill effects or debt that will eventually encompass the deal? Such a deal would not attract much attention. Take the time and effort to understand what makes a particular project or thing work. Your choices determine your outcome in life. Children must be taught that doing a job well will make them much better people and enhance their self-esteem; they must be taught to always respect themselves, respect others and always take responsibility for their actions.

CHAPTER THREE

LIFE BEFORE DIVORCE

Growing up in a family of seven children meant there was never a lot of money, but there was always an abundance of love. My father did construction work and farming. My mother was a housewife who occasionally worked outside of the home. There were not many work opportunities for black females in the 50's and 60's except for domestic work and field work. The same work opportunities applied to the young people as well. In the summer we earned money by working on the farm picking cotton to earn money for back-to-school outfits and supplies.

School was a major part of my life, perhaps even an outlet, as there were not many opportunities for social events during my childhood. The few social events that were available our parents made sure we avoided. I truly enjoyed school, and did very well. In elementary school, I was promoted directly from the third grade to the fifth grade. In junior high and high school, there were four of us in the top academic standing in our class. We competed for the top performance in each class. Any test or quiz on which I did not get an "A" would upset me; I hated to miss a day of school for fear that one of the other girls in class would get ahead of me. This trend continued throughout high school, college and my adult life – I have always try to do my best.

School, church and Sunday school were always a major part of my life growing up. I believe that this contributed to much of my adult character. Children and young people should attend church or some type of religious services, as this might help them to focus on positive things rather than on negative things. Isn't it amazing how God has been taken out of our schools, government, and even our lives, but when disasters happen, we immediately begin to pray to God for help. The Bible teaches us not to kill, steal and to love our neighbors as ourselves, yet it has no place in our children's education.

Common sense has even taken a back seat; many people refuse to take responsibility for anything, blaming others for their mistakes. They believe they have rights and they are the victim. Many tragedies might have been avoided if only our children had been more responsible. We wonder why so many young people have no conscience, or seem not to care and show concern. Many young people don't seem to know right from wrong, and it doesn't seem to bother them to injure or even kill a stranger, classmate or themselves. Isn't it amazing that after God has been pushed into the background and out of our lives, we then wonder why the world is falling apart? Maybe it is time that we reconsider and encourage our children to not be involved in or around detrimental and harmful activities. We need to spend more time and energy learning values that will be much more rewarding and productive.

No matter what your religious background, the basics of loving, sharing and caring for one another is the same. If we learn to care for one another, we would not deliberately hurt anyone. Everyone has a right to their emotions, but anger should not result in cruelty. I still cherish and appreciate some of the values and things that I learned at the church in which I grew up.

When I moved to New York as an adult, I began looking around the area for a church that was close to our home to attend, especially for our son to be able to continue his religious education. After attending a number of churches in the area, we decided on the Prince of Peace Lutheran Church in Cambria Height, New York. The congregation was a good mix of various ethnic backgrounds. Everyone was very nice, and welcomed us warmly. We joined the church, and I have continued to be a member there for over thirty years.

One couple that we met there was Woodie and Clarice Head. We became very good friends, and in many ways they were like my adoptive parents. One day when Mrs. Head and I were doing some shopping for some items for a church activity, a lady referred to me as her daughter, and Mrs. Head didn't correct the lady. Later Mrs. Head started referring to me as her daughter, and after she told her husband the story, he started calling me his daughter as well. This relationship has existed for over twenty years, during which I have been really blessed.

Daddy Head is a retired policeman and is over 90 years old, and Mother Head is over 80 years of age. Neither of them looks much older than 60 years old. They are asked constantly what is their secret? Daddy Head always answered with the statement always treat people as you would like to be treated. I often take Mother Head to church, to the doctor's, and other errands that she needs to make; it is a good relationship.

Another loving family that I met at the Prince of Peach Lutheran Church was Dr. and Marcia Grant, and their three children, Corey, Jihan and Camille. I have known them now over twenty years. When

Camille was confirmed at the church, she asked me to be her sponsor. I said yes, and was glad to stand with her, support and encourage her. Jihan is following in her father's footsteps, and is now studying to become a physician.

Another family that I met was Amanda Jones and her children, Wesley and Sharon. Our children became friends, and grew up together in the church and were involved in the many programs offered at the church. Many members and a number of pastors have come and gone, but many of the families have been affiliated with the church for over thirty years. During this time, I have served on most of the church's committees, and served as chairperson on most. I have served as the Vice President of the Council, President of the Women's Ministry, President of the Senior Choir, an usher and acolyte. My son Keagan served as an acolyte after being confirmed at the Prince of Peace Lutheran Church.

I have always believed that attending a church or religious service may not necessarily help an individual, but I don't believe that it can hurt them. There were only a few social activities that our parents would let us attend during my childhood. I remember many occasions where I would beg and plead for my parents to let me attend a certain activity, especially if it was on a Sunday afternoon. It was understood that if you did not feel well enough to attend Sunday school, you did not feel well enough to attend the social event on Sunday afternoon and would not be permitted to go. These events shaped my life, and have been in part the reason that I have been able to get through some very rough times. These experiences have given me the strength and belief to keep fighting when situations seemed hopeless at times.

Everyone is confronted with different circumstances and various situations in their lives, but whatever your condition is and whatever situation brought you to that predicament or position, there is a way around it, under it, or over it; God will get you through it. Each person's challenges and tests are different, because there is a different lesson that each one of us has to learn. Even if you believe yourself to be a victim of circumstance or consequence of your own actions, you must take responsibility to make the situation better. You alone must be determined to improve your situation, whether it is your education, a job, or a life changing alteration. You may have to start small and then constantly work toward improvement. When I decided to continue my college education, I started taking one or two courses at a time until it was accomplished. Perhaps to get the job you want, you will have to start at a lower position, and work your way up to the top. Confront the situation, and soon you will see the way through the situation. You may not have help, but there will be times that somebody will be there to rescue you; make whatever effort that you can to move forward, because the moment that you settle for less than you deserve, you will get less then you settled for.

You must make the first step, and have patience to continue to fight for your dreams and goals; don't lose sight of where you want to go in life. Never laugh at anyone's dreams. People who do not have dreams and plans will not accomplish very much. Don't sit back and see where your dream will take you, but work to see how far you can take your dream. Have a plan for whatever you want to do. This should be how you work in every phase of your life. Even if your plan does not work out exactly as you wished, you must have a strategy of how you will accomplish the desired mission. Of course there will be disappointments and hard times, and friends and acquaintances will be discouraging and disappointing. Many times people do not want to even hear your dreams. Whenever self–doubt occurs, ask and pray for renewed confidence. Great goals take strength of character, and if something was easy, you would have accomplished it already. You must continue to keep your goal in mind, and your eyes on the prize.

When I graduated from high school, a few of my friends went off to various colleges and universities. Most of us were not able to continue our education because of our financial situation, and others went to local schools. My best friend Carole was more financially prepared for college, as her father was the local mortician. She attended Spelma College in Georgia. After she left for school, and I was not able to attend, I began to feel depressed. A year passed, and I became determined to find a way to attend college. I applied and received a grant based on my good grades, and was able to attend Virginia Union University in Richmond, Virginia. I worked part time to help with my expenses, and attended school there for a year and a half. In the summer, I would come to New York to work and visit with my sister, Shirley. She lived in Middletown, New York. She was the oldest, she always looked out for me and the other younger siblings. I also spent some time with my sister, Jewel, who lived in Brooklyn, New York. There I met my neighbor, Ethan Thomas, who later would become my husband. Thirty years is a long time, especially in a marriage to one person which ends in divorce. In the beginning of our relationship, my friendship with Ethan seemed normal by most standards. We worked together, and established a life for ourselves. I would constantly be encouraging Ethan to try to improve himself by taking a course in school, or joining an organization that would improve his life and status. I tried to get him to limit the time he spent with friends whose characters left a lot to be desired. Instead of listening to me and my suggestions on how to improve himself, he listened to his friends, and would constantly make excuses for not making the necessary efforts to improve his life and behavior. Excuses are the most crippling disease of the human mind. Advice from unproductive people should be ignored; they make no effort to succeed, therefore, they will be the first to tell you how unreachable your goals are. Any time you tolerate mediocrity in others, it increases the mediocrity in yourself. I have observed that one of the important attributes in successful people is they refuse to spend time around negative people.

It is the simple truth that you become like those with whom you closely associate and spend most of your time. If one wishes to move forward from a complacent state of mind, they must change their way of thinking, both in their thoughts and focus. There has to be an entire transformation of thinking, because our thinking has a way of shaping who we are and how we behave. One's thoughts are influenced by one's environment. We must dispense with the old, and focus on the new, to change the direction of our lives, and move forward. The power of positive words can breathe life into a situation, and negative words will suck the life out of a situation.

Ethan spent much of his time gambling, and seemed to think, as did his friends, that drinking and partying was a priority. He did join the Masons, which marked some positive growth since he spent time away from his usual friends. Ethan always seemed to find excuses for not doing something for which he was responsible. Nothing was his responsibility, but he always found the time and energy to do what he wanted, especially hanging out with his friends.

Even though I had encouraged Ethan to continue his education, he never found the time, even though the company he worked for, Con Edison, offered to pay for his education. He had many negative remarks for me, as I pursued my education. His negative comments did not deter me from moving forward. I told him that I firmly believed that nothing replaces or take the place of preparation when you wish to move forward in life and improve yourself. Preparation is essential for success in whatever project or phase in your life. Yesterday's success may not qualify for to-day's or tomorrow's success. It is good to be thankful for what you have achieved, and give thanks to those that assisted you along the way. However, one must not become complacent, for they might find them-selves in the same position, or even falling behind, as others pass them by. Over time, they may even lose what they have accomplished. If you want to achieve and live your dreams, you must work on preparation, learning and networking.

My life was never boring – I continued my educa-tion and working, and before long I was also raising a child. I felt my life was tedious at times. Mother-hood, along with Little League, karate, Cub Scouts, Boy Scouts, and other activities, became almost a second job. I accepted this challenge with enthusi-asm, as Ethan very rarely supported me or shared parental responsibility. When school activities and programs increased for our son, and he needed parental involvement, Ethan started participating less and less, and made excuses for not being able to attend Keagan's various events. The excuses and reasons that he gave did not add up. Many women in this position often justify this feeling by telling themselves that they are wrong, or maybe their man is not lying. I desperately wanted to believe Ethan, and tried to ignore that little voice, my sixth sense. No matter what it is, a sense, a thought in the back of your head, or a soft whisper, listen to it! If you suspect that something is not right with your spouse when their activities and routine starts to vary from their normal behavior, listen to it! When their reasons and excuses just don't quite make sense, listen to it! No matter what you suspect, there is always some reason for any change.

Eventually, I had to ask some questions to try to understand what was going on, but all I got was ridiculous explanations. Ethan's answers didn't quite make sense, and he became very defensive and I could tell that he was lying. I started to do my research and found that he was seeing other women behind my back. Still, I gave him a chance to be honest, and watched his face in amazement as he struggled to come up with a lie to cover up his behavior. Ethan was very argumentative and a chronic liar. He would very quickly try to turn the blame back to me or some other person.

If you work at cultivating respect in your relationship rather than focusing just on the romance and dreams you've had, you can objectively decide to move on before a lot of energy and valuable time is lost in a bad relationship, or even worse, before you are abused. Face the reality, when you suspect something is wrong, it usually is. Don't jump to the wrong conclusion, but do some research. Get the facts and remember, your sixth sense is never wrong, listen to your sixth sense.

It turned out that Ethan was involved in adulterous affairs, one after another. He tried to cover his sins with lie after lie, and when I tried to confront him about his behavior, he would resort to cursing loudly, as if that would win the argument. This was how we communicated, right up to the ugly divorce.

I was working for the New York Telephone Company, and by the time my thirty-year career was over, the company also went through many changes. Their name changed several times, from the New York Telephone Company, to Bell Atlantic, to NYNEX, and to the present, Verizon. Ethan began employment with Con Edison the same year I started work with the New York Telephone Company. During his first years with Con Edison, Ethan more or less met most of his financial and other responsibilities. He was responsible for the mortgage, since we had obtained our house mortgage through Con Edison. I was responsible for the rest of the bills: utilities, electric, gas, oil, food, furniture, etc. All of Ethan's extra money went towards his gambling and womanizing, which he continued to deny each time that he was confronted.

Like any gambler, Ethan believed that he would eventually strike it big, and win a lot of money, even though he was constantly told that it does not happen this way. If gambling really does pay off, why are there so many people suffering the ill effects of this curse, and thousands of others are trying to get help to break the habits of their addiction? During this time, Ethan continued to lose the money that he should have saved for his half of the bills, and living conditions became very uncomfortable. I had to close our joint checking account, since he would write checks and withdraw money for his personal follies.

Ethan continued to make mistakes, and I tried to maintain and display a normal life. I dropped his name from our bank accounts, so that I could use that money to pay household bills, and to prevent him from using the money for his personal follies. He worked with Con Edison for a number of years, until he was eventually terminated. Even after he left Con Edison, he continued to receive unemployment benefits, which he used for his addictions instead of assisting with responsibilities and obligations.

I learned that I was doing the same thing that many other women do when faced with similar situations. I kept hoping that things will work out and improve, but I knew deep down that they wouldn't. I didn't want to face the facts and remove myself from this toxic relationship. Many women maintain a façade, realizing that they are being taken advantage of, but do nothing to stop it. Perhaps you don't see the problem at first, but then something happens that helps you see the light. I like to believe that this is God's intervention. As you continue to put things in perspective, you will see how people will do what you permit, and you are the one who needs to change the situation. Are you holding onto a harmful partner, relationships, habits or activities that seem to be impossible to let go? It is hard to see beyond your present state, but believe in God, and He will bring you to a better position and place. If you continue to operate in the same manner as you always have, you will probably get the same results you always have. You need to change the way you are doing things. Make the decision to let it go, let them go, let him or her go. Let go of whatever or whoever it is, so you will be able to move forward and restructure your life in a positive manner.

CHAPTER FOUR

SHAME ON BIASES AND PREJUDICES

Soon after I started working as a service clerk with The New York Telephone Company, I was promoted to facility clerk. I worked hard, and was as pleasant as possible, and in two short years I was promoted to assistance manager. Two years later I was promoted to manager. I worked various locations around Brooklyn and Queens.

There were many obstacles, frustrations and prejudices that were sometimes obvious, while others were camouflaged. During my lifetime, I have encountered many of life's experiences. Sometimes kindness is taken for weakness and silence for speechless. My confidence was considered conceit, and my success accidental. A mistake was considered defeat and my intelligence was often minimized as merely having potential. My hard work and educational accomplishment was often overlooked, and in the process of standing up for myself, I was considered too defensive.

Dignity and respect should be expected by every person in the work place; one needs to play by the rules to earn the ability to make rules. A lot of prejudices and racial bias still exist today. Insensitive remarks, disrespectful and racial comments are only comical and funny to those who share the same ignorant views. Often the victims of these biases are later found to be not at all as others had viewed them. Many times those who make unkind remarks are guilty of many of the same flaws that they notice in the other person. The unkind persons are not only ignorant, but are insecure; they do not value their own standards, which often stems from lack of accomplishment and education. Still, these despicable beliefs cloud our judgment, and are passed from one generation to the next. We've conquered the atom, but not our prejudices.

Most everybody has had a unpleasant experience with someone, but this does not justify judging an entire group or race by the actions of a few.

The existence of prejudice and racial bias was proven in an experiment conducted by a certain high school. The class was comprised of various races, cultures and backgrounds. Certain students of a particular ethnic background made derogatory remarks about students of another race and culture. Although they knew it made these students feel uncomfortable and upset, they continued to make fun of them. When the team conducting the experiment confronted these students, they realized the hurt they had caused. They were asked how they would feel if similar remarks were made about them. They answered that it would make them feel very bad and unhappy. They then realize how hurtful the remarks were, and couldn't come up with any reason why they made those remarks in the first place. They later admitted that the students who they had been making fun of had always associated with them in a positive way.

These students admitted that the feelings and behavior against these students was passed on to them by parents and relatives, and they had learned to refer to people of different races and cultures this way.

A baby is born without any preconceived ideas, a clean slate, and learns from their environment. However, when one becomes of age, it is his or her responsibility to change and correct their behavior when you know something is wrong. A responsible person does not continue to do what is wrong when they have learned better. Isn't it ironic that when one person is being discriminated against, others often stand by and laugh or say nothing? Yet, when the direction of the humiliation turns against them, they quickly find that it is not a nice feeling at all. No matter what culture you are, being discriminated against never feels funny or pleasant.

The young people at this school immediately admitted what they had been doing was wrong, and apologized and hugged the students they had been making fun of. They promised to correct their behavior, and to discuss it with their parents and relatives to let them know this type of behavior should not be justified. Behavior is learned and practiced in the home. Our background and circumstances may have influenced who we are, but we are still responsible for who we become. The students learned a lot by just reflecting on how they would feel if they were treated in such manner. They then started to consider the other students' feelings, and begin to treat them with respect as they would like to be treated.

The cycle has to be broken, and it must start with each one of us. The students in this story eventually all became friends. It is not necessary to confront, but to make your point in a polite manner. People are people, no matter in what country, race or cultural they originated. Exhibiting preconceived biases and prejudices against other cultures and races limit opportunities that are necessary for all to compete on an equal basis. Derogatory remarks and anger is usually a condition where the tongue works faster than the mind. Someone once said, "Before passing judgment, walk a mile in the other person's shoes." You must be comfortable with yourself before you can really care and love someone else. We all live on this earth to do our best, we are all made the same way, and all have the basic needs and wants.

If we make more of an effort to unite, we could accomplish so much more. The things that make us alike are much greater than those things that separate us. We must realize that there is more that unites us than divides us. The difference between each person is what makes us unique, and we should appreciate, embrace and learn from other cultures. Differences do not make anyone superior or inferior to the other, nor do these differences mean that one is truly any different. Since we are more alike than different, wouldn't it be to our advantage to work together? Together we could accomplish numerous tasks and move many more mountains. This we need to keep in mind.

Step outside of your own little world, and find out what others are doing and thinking. It has been said never to underestimate your opponent, but you should never underestimate anyone. We can all learn from each other; you can even learn from babies and small children in some of the amazing things that they do and say. You must be willing to open up and learn new ideas, and appreciate that each person is basically the same. Some people are exceptional, some are average and some are not so smart. This is the same all over the world, because that is how God made us. Love knows no color, and love does not hurt.

Whatever roadblocks that you encounter in your life, take them as a challenge. They may slow you down or temporary deter you from your goals, but don't give up; be persistent. Don't let critics deter you; don't even listen to them. You must get on with the job that needs to be done. So-called friends that don't help you reach your goals are not truly your friends. Friends will either encourage you to stretch your vision, or not be a hindrance to your dreams. Suppress your fear; it can be one of the greatest problems to overcome. Sometimes compromise is necessary to get where you are going. This doesn't mean that you have to sacrifice your integrity. Your most prized possession is your integrity. You must be willing to open your mind to change, but not let new ideals dilute or change your principles and values.

Anger, cursing and foul language will not help you accomplish your goal. It is okay to feel angry, to cry and get upset, because we are only human. However, you must turn that anger to positive and constructive energy, pick yourself up and charge forward to achieve your goals. You must not become bitter. Feel free to disagree if their point or view is different than yours; this is your right. You will earn much more respect if you have a valid point to present as well. If you follow and always agree with the crowd, you will lose your identity. A combination of good ideas tends to work much better than a single idea most of the time. I have experienced this, and have come to be a better person by being friends with people of different cultures and races.

In a work situation, as well as in any life situation, you should do an evaluation of the situation. If you have more pros than cons, then you are a winner, if there are more cons than pros, you may want to re-evaluate the situation before a final decision is made. Each and every situation has pros and cons: a relationship, a marriage, a job and most of life. Take the time to add up the pros and the cons, and if the pros outnumber the cons, you might just have a great situation. However, if the opposite occurs, you should seriously consider some changes. Why remain in a negative situation when any option or choice might improve your situation, and maybe save your life?

CHAPTER FIVE

BATTLEGROUND OF A SPOUSE'S BEHAVIOR

After Ethan was terminated from Con Edison for his bad behavior, he quickly depleted his unemployment benefits and severance pay by supporting his bad habits. He was constantly encouraged to seek some other type of employment, for even a little money was better than nothing. I needed help with some of the household responsibilities. Someone said, "A half of loaf is better then no loaf at all." I helped him gain employment with the New York Telephone Company, which was a temporary position for two years. He later decided to leave the position and go into the taxi business. I continued to assist him, and we took out a loan and purchased a Medallion and Yellow Taxi. At first Ethan did about as well as could be expected, and seemed to make a good effort. Unfortunately, he was soon back to his old habits.

After only a couple of years, Ethan decided to relocate to North Carolina. Of course I was very apprehensive about this, and wondered about his sanity. I asked him what his plan was, since we were not prepared financially to move, especially when neither of us would have a job waiting for us there. We still had an outstanding loan for the Medallion, but Ethan argued that many of his friends were relocating to the South. As usual, he seemed to be living in a fantasy world.

I realized that if I accompanied him to North Carolina, I was most likely going to be manipulated into supporting him. I decided that I was not going to continue to be taken for granted. I had a great job, and I was also attending Adelphi University at night to get my degree in Business Administration. I could not justify leaving everything I had going for me, especially when I had no idea what would await me in North Carolina. I told him I was not going.

Approximately a month later, Ethan informed me that he had decided he was going to relocate to North Carolina alone. I wished him well, for I had already made up my mind that I was staying. During this time, my life became even more complicated; our son was in trouble. Keagan had been accused of rape.

Two women who were older than he was had picked him up from his home in Queens, and drove him to Brooklyn; they wanted to meet his cousin. One of these girls was a previous girlfriend. Needless to say, this turned into an over thirteen year nightmare. According to court documents, they visited the cousin's apartment, where they played video-games and drank beer. Keagan's ex-girlfriend went into one room to sleep, and Keagan followed. His cousin took the other girl to another room, where they had sex. Later this girl claimed that she had been raped by both Keagan and his cousin. Keagan's cousin admitted that he and the girl had had consensual sex, and not Keagan. DNA tests proved Keagan innocent, but we continued to fight this nightmare through years of injustice. I knew that dealing with Keagan's situation and an impending divorce was not going to be an easy task.

Keagan had been attending college, and was working for Con Edison before this incident occurred. He had passed both the NYPD test and the Correction Officer's test. We later were told that this girl has accused other men of rape, and that she was looking for money. She must have assumed that Keagan's family had money, as she saw Keagan driving a Pathfinder SUV. We felt that with these witnesses to the girl's motive would be helpful to our case. Yet, when it came time to testify in court, these people conveniently did not appear. Both girls who were involved that night already had a child each, and were much older than Keagan.

Prior to this nightmare, things had seemed to be heading in the right direction. I could not understand why these things were happening to me. I had always tried to do the right thing by helping others, treating others with respect, and studying and believing in the Bible. One particular Bible story that I would relate to was the story of Job and his struggles, but ultimately his success. I encouraged Keagan to read the story of Joseph in the Bible, where his brothers sold him into slavery, but later they were forced to come and bow down to him, as he was their means of survival. I decided that my trials may be a test of my faith, and one has to get through the rainstorm to get to the sunshine. As my life continued to fall apart around me, I started to think that God was maybe working something in my life with the challenges. At this point I knew I needed to put my entire trust in God, and that He would get me through these rough times. I kept telling myself that there is a reason for everything. We may not understand at the time why, and may never understand why, but there is a reason for everything, and God knows what it is. Then I told myself, "If God got me to it, God will get me through it."

Ethan continued to live in North Carolina during this time in an apartment, and worked as a bus driver. We had occasional communication. He insisted that I come to visit him, and reluctantly I traveled to North Carolina, hoping to make some sense of my marriage. He was, just as I had pictured, living in an apartment with only basic necessities. He was still the same selfish man, and demanded that I help support him. He asked for money to help pay his rent, and I regrettably gave it to him. I suggested he accompany me to counseling, to help deal with his gambling, drinking, and womanizing. I tried to help him see that he had to change his behavior if he wanted to save his marriage and improve his life. His kept telling me, "I don't need any counseling, you are the one that needs counseling." I agreed that we both should go, but no counseling ever took place. Several months passed, and Ethan's fantasy of North Carolina had not turned out as he had hoped, and he tried to get me to allow him to return to New York.

We discussed his returning to New York, and eventually agreed on some basic guidelines. We agreed that his behavior would change, he would be more supportive at home in financial and domestic matters, and that his womanizing would cease. I hoped that someday he would go with me to counseling.

After Ethan had been home a few weeks, he seemed to be sticking to our guidelines. He decided to start his own gardening business, and this seemed to work out for awhile. Unfortunately, he soon started to revert back to his old ways, and the real Ethan surfaced. Before long he was gambling, drinking and smoking marijuana once again. Some of his customers begin to complain that he had overcharged them, and was not doing a quality job. As his business fell apart, I encouraged him return to his job at the New

York Telephone Company, which was now known as NYNEX. I spoke to a person in Human Resources, and made arrangements for him to return to work doing some of the same responsibilities that he had previously performed. It should not have surprised me that he did not return. He told me that he needed time to do his landscaping and gardening business, but the truth was that he didn't want anything stopping him from gambling in the middle of the day. Not only did he gamble most of the day, but late into the night.

I was right back to the same situation I had been before. I was still working as a manager for NYNEX, attending Adelphi University in the evening, and trying to work on Keagan's case. Needless to say, this whole situation was taking its toll on me. Still, I was determined to finish my degree, which I did. I graduated from Adelphi University with my B.S. Degree in Business Administration. Ethan attended the graduation ceremony, but only because one of my girlfriends made him feel guilty. My friends made a point of the hard work that I had put into this degree, and that he should be very proud. The day went well, but it wasn't long after graduation that Ethan's derogative remarks and jealousy increased. A few months after graduating from Adelphi University, I enrolled at CW Post College, and began pursuing my Master Degree in Physiology.

I tried to stay positive for myself and others, but I broke down and cried many times. It seemed like everything was closing in on me, and I did not know what to do or to whom to turn. I believe if you need to cry, you should allow yourself to do so. If you have to scream, then scream. If you have to yell, then yell. Allow yourself to release some tension and pressure, then regroup and move on. Don't wallow in self-pity, because the most worthless emotion is self-pity. Don't look for sympathy from others, but allow yourself to find friends that can empathize with you and encourage you. One of the biggest distractions in life is focusing only on the things that you are going through rather than finding a solution to your problems. Do what's necessary, then you will be able to continue past your problems. You have to be the one to re-examine the situation, and look for a solution.

Just because somebody is there for you to talk to, doesn't mean they are well-meaning, or will be able to help you in the end. Most people love to listen to other people's problems for gossip. You should always be mindful about what you share with people, as I have found out. A story can be twisted into a completely negative spin, and used against you. I have never been one to discuss my personal business with anyone. Ask yourself, *"Why is this person interested in my problems, and how can they help me?"* Listen to your sixth sense before answering. Many times some of my co-workers would be upset about what somebody else was saying about their personal business. I would ask them, how did these people learn about it in the first place. They would almost always answer, "Oh, I mention it to someone." If you share intimate details with somebody who is not trustworthy, you can only blame yourself when it is spread around. Learn from your mistakes. During my lifetime, I have made sure I have never passed on anything somebody told me in confidence. The tongue is the deadliest weapon in the world. You may have a few friends that you know are genuine and have your best interest at heart; these you will be able to share your heart with. Otherwise, take your concerns and problems to the Lord in prayer. The most powerful channel of communication is prayer. You must remember that tough times do not last, but tough people do. God will get you through.

CHAPTER SIX

FAMILY, FRIENDS, AND A POLITICIAN'S POWER

France Amey was one of my truest friends; she was my neighbor and co-worker. As I was a manager in various office locations, she was one of my assistant managers. We had both a good working relationship and a wonderful friendship outside of work. We were able to keep these two relationships separate. She respected my position, and worked hard just because we were friends, without any selfish motive. Few people ever experience such a friendship, because it is hard for most people to separate business and friendship, and this creates problems for both parties. Business and friendship must be kept separate.

Audrey Ballard was another good friend who I meet some years later through NYNEX. She was one of the administrative clerks in my office when I worked for Verizon as a consultant. Most people can claim they had at least one person that they are great friends with. If you are lucky enough to have many of these kind of friends, this is a rare and wonderful gift. I remember that my mother would say, "You can count true friends on one hand, with the majority of your fingers left over."

True friends are like quiet angels who lift you to your feet when your wings are having trouble remembering how to fly. A true friend will be there when you need a shoulder to cry on, and will often cry with you. A true friend respects you for being creative, and for thinking outside the box. They will accept you just the way you are. Good friends are like stars, you don't always see them or quite know where they are, but you know they are there for you. In true friendship, you don't take the advantage, you give the advantage. True friendship is the golden thread that binds our hearts together. True friendship will forever be true, because people will still be people. When you find a true friend, value this friendship, and don't let something insignificant like a little squabble damage a good friendship. When a disagreement occurs, deal with the current situation. Don't bring up the past. When you realize that you have made a mistake, take immediately steps to correct it. A hug is a great gift, and one size fit all; it can be given for any occasion, and it's easy to exchange. It is human nature for people to ask questions about your affairs and business, as if they have your best interest at heart, while all the time plotting a devious venture. When someone asks you a question that you'd rather not answer, just smile and ask, "Why do you want to know?"

During this difficult time in my life, friends and family stood by me with whatever support they could give. Still the weight of my problems were heavy on my shoulders. At the same time I was trying to get justice for Keagan, I had to obtain a lawyer for my divorce proceedings as well. The trial took place for our son, and even with all of the efforts we had made on his behalf, and even though the DNA test proved him innocent, he was still sentenced to serve time. The presiding judge indicated that he wanted to make an example of Keagan and his cousin. Years later, while I was still pursuing justice in this case, I found out that this judge had passed away, after another somewhat public rape case had convicted the wrong guys, I directed my energy and time to try to find out how to get justice for Keagan. I obtained another lawyer, who was very professional and knew the system well, and still our appeal was denied. There was a second appeal after I obtained another lawyer that was recommended to me, and again it was denied.

During this time, I wrote letters to congressmen, senators, representatives, commissioners, the governor, chairpersons of various departments and organizations, as well as the president of the United States, to ask for help to correct this injustice. I knew that the politicians would probably respond in a political manner; still I hoped and prayed that someone would look at the facts of this case, and help us get justice. President Clinton answered my letter, and indicated that since this was state matter, not a federal matter, he would refer this case to the state officials. I appreciated him responding at least.

Even though I knew it was a state case, I tried everyone that I could think of that could be of assistance. Governor George Pataki also answered, and indicated that the case would be referred to the proper agencies and commissions, which would look into the matter. Senator Hillary Clinton also answered, and suggested the agencies and commissions to whom we should get in touch. Congresswoman Barbara Clark, also answered and wrote a letter on our behalf to the Governor and the Department of Corrections. Senator D'Amato did not respond to our letter. When he ran for re-election the next year, he lost. I couldn't help but think that God was still in the equation. Congressman Meeks and his assistant Patrick Jenkins were very helpful in helping me write letters and contact various departments and correctional institutions to correct some situations that occurred with our son.

Two different correctional facilities that Keagan was incarcerated at didn't have updated records, and they insisted that Keagan attend GED Courses. He explained to them that he had not only graduated from high school, but had been attending college. I contacted both the Bayside High School and Nassau College where Keagan had attended, and paid to have the transcripts sent to where he was being incarcerated. Still there seemed to be a lack of coordination and organization as to what was going on. Nobody seemed to be receiving the transcripts, and the records weren't being updated. One of the officers at the prison was very helpful in helping to finally correct this problem.

We were told of the Brooklyn Law School, and how they would take on cases like our son's. I contacted the Brooklyn Law School, and spoke with Professor Hallenstein. He said he couldn't promise anything, but that they would try to help us. He explained what cases they would work on, and that they did their own DNA testing, even though in our case the DNA test was already done and had come back negative.

In the Brooklyn Law School, the students take on only certain cases, and didn't know if our case would be chosen as their class project. Professor Hallenstein showed us compassion, and encouraged us to keep in communication. During this time we also contacted the Benjamin Cardozo School of Law, but they were not able to take our case. We made arrangements with a variety of community groups and organizations that presented character witnesses on Keagan's behalf, and asked Governor Pataki to look at the facts fairly, but this turned out to be yet another political "no."

Senator Daniel Moynihan was helpful in getting our son transferred back to a facility that was approximately four hours away instead of the eight hour drive to the facility he was currently being held at. Various friends and family members would drive with me to visit Keagan. Ethan and I went to visit our son together a few times. As Ethan's behavior and our marriage deteriorated, I found myself visiting our son alone. Still, I was determined that I would continue to fight for justice for our son, even if I had to do it by myself.

Having Keagan transferred to a closer facility was truly a gift from God, as it had been difficult for me to drive over eight hours one way to visit my son. As if my life wasn't hard enough at this point, I had suffered a serious car accident, and sustained injuries to my knee, back and neck. Traveling became very difficult of me, and a shorter drive was very much appreciated. Specific visiting hours also made it difficult to visit, so I could only visit Keagan on the weekends, due to work and school. I continued to fight for Keagan as tensions grew in my marriage to Ethan.

CHAPTER SEVEN
INFIDELITY AND DIVORCE DRAMA

As Ethan's infidelity became more and more apparent, I decided to protect myself sexually, and moved into another bedroom. It was one thing when I merely suspected his unfaithfulness, but when the evidence is undeniable, I would've been a complete fool if I had not taken action to protect myself. There are many sexually transmittable diseases including HIV/AIDS, which is a serious matter to be concerned with. As time passed, more and more evidence of his many affairs became obvious. There were many occasions when Ethan would be out late, or even out all night. He would tell me that he had been out with the guys, or at his cousin's house, playing cards and gambling. Still, I overhead numerous telephone conversations that he had been seeing other women during that time. I felt sick to my stomach as I would sometimes overhear him discuss intimate details with his lovers on the telephone. I was devastated that he could find time to take these women out, yet when I asked him to attend a play, concert or even go out to dinner, he would always say that he didn't like doing those things or he was doing something with his friends.

During this time, I attended many Broadway plays, concerts and performances; these were my way of maintaining some of my sanity. I refused to allow my circumstances to dictate my happiness, and I took the time to take care of myself. My girlfriends would often accompany me, and we had a wonderful time. I didn't want to look back and resent this time as being lost. Once you are aware of your situation, you are responsible for any changes that need to be made to the situation. You may not be able to change people, but you can change your situation. Some circumstances and situations can't be changed immediately, but you can change them. Instead of wallowing in your self-pity, focus on changing your life for the better.

In June of 2002, my sister Dorothy performed in the play "To Kill a Mockingbird" at the Kennedy Center in Washington D.C. She was a part time actress, and I thought for once that Ethan would want to go and see the play to show our support. Sadly, Ethan had no interest in the play and refused to go with me. Dorothy and the cast traveled across the country performing, and had also performed the play in both Israel and England. A girlfriend and I drove all the way from New York to Washington D.C. to see the play and support my sister. My sister Shirley also flew down from upstate New York to see the play. Dorothy's performance was amazing, and everyone thoroughly enjoyed themselves. I returned home and resumed my routine.

My friends and family had no idea of the extent of the hell I was experiencing at the time. However, they knew enough to know that I was living a nightmare. Perhaps some of my stubbornness to completely give up on Ethan stemmed from my childhood; I can remember many times trying to work out a family situation in the family. I was never one discuss my personal problems or gossip among my family or friends. My generation has often exhibited a certain facade, indicating that things were better than they really were. When my friends or family learned more about my personal crisis, they couldn't understand how I had dealt with so much at one time. They claimed I was an extraordinary person to have been able to cope, but I told them that I prayed a lot, and believed in God. I knew if He got me to this, He would get me through it. God knows best, and He will get you through whatever you are going through in your life.

In December of 1992, I received a call that my father was very ill, and now I needed to find the time and strength to go and visit him. My family was very close, and I wanted to be there for him. While I was visiting my family, Ethan remained in New York. I hesitated to tell our son of his grandfather's illness. Keagan had already been through so much, and I wanted to spare him additional heartache. Still, I knew I had to tell him because he had a close relationship with his grandfather. He had lived with his grandparents for two years when he was a small boy. I had sent him there because I knew he would be safe, and loved and cared for; I had had such a difficult time finding a good babysitter, and because I was working full-time, I could not care for him.

Keagan was very upset after hearing the news of his grandfather. He talked to me about the good times he had had with his grandparents, uncles, aunts and cousins. He attended school there with his cousins, Edward and Frances. His teacher had been my sister, Alice. She was an excellent teacher, and made sure that each student's homework was done, and disciplined them when needed. Many parents would request that their children be placed in her class, as she had earned a reputation of caring and concern for the students. My whole family had been involved in raising Keagan, Edward and Frances. My sister Dorothy enrolled them in various activities, amusements and of course Sunday school and Church. My brother Ray and sister Jewel never had any children, but they loved and treated every niece and nephew as if they were their own child.

My family was very close, and was always helping one another. My brother Ray helped start the family business where we sold plants, flowers, gardening supplies and had a mini grocery story called the "Mini Mart." As anyone who has started their own business can attest, it demanded long hours and gave very little profit if any. Still each member of our family worked hard to help keep it going. There is nothing to compare with a loving and caring family. Many people feel that they are expendable, and nobody would miss them if they died, but if one is part of a close family, they would feel the loss for the rest of their lives. Sadly, many of use treat our friends and even mere acquaintances with more respect and love than we do our own flesh and blood. Someone said the word FAMILY means: (F)ather (A)nd (M)other (I) (L)ove (Y)ou.

My father did not recover from his illness, and passed away on Christmas Day. Ever since that day, Christmas has not been quite the the same for our family. After burying my father, I returned to New York, and continued pursuing justice for Keagan.

For almost five years I had struggled with the inevitable end of my marriage, and my fight for Keagan's justice. Ethan's affairs were becoming more and more apparent, and while he continued to deny his adultery, he made less of an effort to keep them secret. For some time now, I had been recording our telephone line, and was appalled by the things my husband was telling various women. When I would confront Ethan, he would threaten to sue me for breach of privacy. I was devastated how he would be so cold towards me, talking to other women as if I were a problem that needed to be solved. He promised the different women he was sleeping with exotic trips and rendezvous, yet he couldn't find the time to take me out for a simple dinner. A survey once stated that 90% of married men that have affairs do not end up with the "other" woman. They talk about their marriage as some kind of imprisonment of which they are not able to get out of for some reason. However, they still find the time to be just charming enough to get whatever physical desires they wish from these other women. If a guy cheats to be with another woman, he will almost always cheat when he's with her.

If a man really wanted be with someone and spend his life with them, wouldn't he get a divorce and move on with you in his life? Anybody who cheats is not being honest, especially with themselves, their spouse, and their family and friends. Ironically, as I am writing this book, Ethan is not with any of the woman he was sleeping with while married to me. Such empty promises that he made to both them and me. What happened?

In a situation of infidelity, what hurts the most is not just the betrayal of your marriage vows, but how you feel like a fool for not seeing what everybody else knew about. With Ethan's affairs, many of the neighbors knew many of the details, but I only had a gut feeling about what was going on. Ethan started a relationship with our next-door neighbor, and would tell everybody that he was just helping her, when he was actually meeting her for sex. It was almost impossible to talk to Ethan as he refused to admit to anything he was doing. I repeatedly tried to give him an opportunity to come clean about his actions, but he seemed compelled to justify himself with the most creative stories. I told him that I did not deserve this type of treatment, and was not going to fight for a marriage that he was never going to respect. He thought he could continue to have the appearance of a happily married family man, while continuing on with his unfaithfulness. I told him that I wanted a divorce, and that I had had enough of both his actions and his deceit.

Ethan realized that the facade of our marriage was crumbing, and he would not longer be able to play the part of both a single playboy and a married man. He told me that he wanted to be the one who filed for divorce, which was fine with me. Granting a divorce from Ethan was still not an easy process. It took two trials, one involving a jury, and many appearances in family court for over five years before our separation was final. Ethan seemed to try to make everything extremely difficult for me, and refused to be civil about anything. The divorce was finally final in October 2002.

The years leading up to my divorce were a bumpy ride in every sense of the word. For over two years there had been no communication between us, even though we were still living under the same roof, albeit in separate bedrooms. I had tried to talk to him several times to try to come to a rational settlement, but this had failed. When I would make even a little progress towards what I thought would be fair, he would eventually revert back to his old behavior, and come up with ridiculous demands. He wanted me pay for his attorney fees as well as spousal support. For over ten years, he had not contributed even one dime toward our mortgage, or any other household bills. Yet, he continued to live with me, came and went as he pleased, and all the time leading his double life. When I confronted him about his lack of responsibility in our joint finances, he told me that he had not wanted to live in New York, and since I was the one who wanted to stay, he was not going to pay anything. I reminded him that all adults, no matter where they live, have to pay either a rent or mortgage to continue to reside in that place. He was so determined to destroy me, that every rational part of him was no longer in control; it was useless.

I asked a mutual friend of ours to try to talk with Ethan, hoping that she could help mediate our situation without the additional cost of lawyer fees. This friend met with Ethan and went over the housing situation. I had had an appraisal of the house, and I offered to pay Ethan a fair share based on his contributions. Our friend agreed with this arrangement, I could no longer avoid going to court, since it was impossible to negotiate with Ethan, and our divorce had already turned into a three-year nightmare. My mental, physical and financial exhaustion were unbelievable at this point. I was so frustrated with Ethan for not making a sensible agreement, because the only people who were winning in our case was the lawyers. Every telephone call, document, court visit and any time a lawyer was used cost me a lot of money. I didn't understand why two rational adults couldn't work out a civil agreement. Many times in a divorce, one or both of the parties are so consumed with jealousy, envy and selfishness, that this prevents them from being rational or civil. I felt angry, almost like a crime had been committed against me. I was basically being robbed of the thousands of dollars that were being given to the lawyers; I knew this money could have been used for many other things for which I desparately needed money.

Even after our divorce was final, Ethan did everything he could to harass me and make my life miserable. Once he realized that I knew the details of his affairs, he decided to get a restraining order against me, as he anticipated that I would confront these women. He told our next-door neighbor, whom he had been seeing, not to speak to me. I notice that any greetings had ceased, and all communication had stopped. Even to this day this neighbor still refuses to speak to me. Before Ethan began his affair with the neighbor, we spoke regularly, and had the basic neighborly chats. It is true that I would have probably talked with her about Ethan and her relationship, but it is just as well not to aggravate myself and waste even more energy on such common fools.

Not long after we filed for divorce, I was forced to get a restraining order against Ethan as well. Still he continued to try to intimidate me, and the police were called on various occasions. On one occasion, he removed my clothes out of the closet in the master bedroom and placed them in a chair in the smaller bedroom where I had been sleeping. He explained that since I refused to sleep in the same bedroom as he, he was throwing my clothes out of his living space. Another time, he invited some of his friends to have a cookout, which quickly turned into a very loud affair with loud music and many drunk people. I called the police again, and things finally settled down. Ethan was determined to make my life a living hell, but I was determined to let him know that he was not going to intimidate me by any of his methods.

As our court date was approaching, depositions were taken from both Ethan and I, which turned out to be another two days of unbelievable drama. On the day of our court date, a jury was selected, and the trial finally got underway. Ethan was trying to get spousal support, and as such, accused me of abandoning the marriage. I provided proof of Ethan's affairs with various women, and that I had moved out of the bedroom to protect myself from any possible sexual diseases. Our next-door neighbor testified that Ethan had only helped her with maintenance work around her house, and that they had never had any sexual or romantic relationship.

This testimony actually worked in my behalf. Ethan's lawyer asked our neighbor the basic questions that they had rehearsed, but when it came time for my lawyer to cross-examine her, it became clear that she was not telling the truth. He first confirmed her home telephone number as well as the telephone number where she worked. The local line usage indicated that Ethan had called this lady about four to seven times each day for a period of over three months. My lawyer asked our neighbor about these calls, but she maintained that my husband and she had discussed gardening work and repairs around her house. My lawyer confirmed that it truly did not take seven calls just to discuss work around the house. After this display, it was obvious that something else had been indeed going on. After two days of court hearings, the jury voted in my favor; I was not guilty of abandonment.

Even though we still had a settlement to be made, I thanked God that the jury was able to see through the lies, and recognize the truth. When you are at your lowest moments, and everything seems to be falling apart, believe in God that He will help the truth prevail. Some situations take longer than others to work out, but keep in mind that during this time, situations are developing, and puzzles are being solved of which you might not even be aware. Truth always triumphs in the end.

After Ethan lost his hope of spousal support, he became more determined to make my life miserable. I tried several times to talk to him sensibly so that we could come to an agreement, and he and I could go our separate ways and get on with our lives. Still, I was unable to reach an agreement with him. Ethan decided to subpoena a mutual friend to testify at the hearing about an investment that she and I had made years earlier, but had gone bankrupt. Even though we had lost everything, Ethan insisted that there had to be some finances from which he could benefit.

It was stated at the hearing that the company that we had invested in went bankrupt and there was no money for him or us. This was just one more of Ethan's schemes that didn't work and was just unnecessary torture that he put me through. Family court also seemed like a ridiculous nightmare. The buildings and facilities were old, and in much need of repairs. The whole scene was depressing and humiliating, with Ethan and my personal matters exposed. Still, this drama continued for another two years.

After the divorce was final, Ethan was now free to move back to North Carolina as he had wanted. We still shared the same house until he was able to move out. He continued to treat me with disrespect, but I had made up my mind, and prayed for strength to not say anything to him. I hoped that he would be out of my life as soon as possible.

The day came when he finally moved out, and after he gave me his key, I said to him, "God go with you." I truly wished him well. I immediately called a locksmith to change all the locks in the house. I knew that if Ethan ever returned to New York, he would most likely feel free to enter the property, especially if I was not home. It is important to avoid unnecessary aggravation and headaches when possible.

While I was grateful to be out of my dysfunctional marriage, I now I had to pay my ex-husband his share of our property. I had to go further in debt to pay him, and while I am still struggling to pay my responsibilities each month, it was worth the peace of mind to have him out of my life; I have been able to move on with my life. I know God will continue to get me through whatever is ahead of me. If you are in a dysfunctional marriage, it is important to try to make things work through counseling and communication. However, if divorce is inevitable, try to be civil towards one another, especially if there are young children. Divorce lawyers are more than happy to extend the proceedings as long as possible, as they are usually concerned more about their pocketbooks than your divorce becoming final. I know from experience that when one party is stubborn and vindictive, you may have to pay dearly to finalize the procedure, and be able to move on with your life.

With Ethan finally moved out, my focus returned to pursuing justice for Keagan, and putting my life back together. My house was in need of many repairs. The roof needed to be replaced, the garage door needed work, and other things needed to be done that had been neglected during the divorce. Ethan had refused to do any repairs, since he maintained that he had wanted to live in North Carolina, and that I was the one wanted to live there. I made the arrangements for these repairs to be made, although not without a considerable amount of expense. I arranged to have a friend's son help me with chores and gardening, until I was able to get a gardener. It felt good to have my life back in my own hands.

CHAPTER EIGHT

KEAGAN'S NEW DAY

After years of prayers, letter writing, enormous lawyer fees, many trips and a continued fight for justice, Keagan was finally released. His cousin Emilio and I picked him up at the facility. The trip to get Keagan seemed to take forever as I was full of anticipation to see my son. When I asked Keagan how he felt, he was just as in shock after all we had gone through for his justice. We were finally bringing him home! We stopped at a restaurant on the way back to have lunch. Keagan was beaming with gratitude to be coming home. He was going to have many adjustments as he returned to normal life. Keagan has been successful at making these adjustments; I am sure his efforts, religious beliefs and family structure played a major role in his ability to succeed. During his incarceration, Keagan's educational status was eventually corrected after numerous trips, phone calls and letters. He was able to enroll in some courses at the prison, and received some certifications. Since coming home, he has now become a certified personal trainer and a real estate agent. He is presently pursuing additional education and interests as well.

Keagan knew that he had been incarcerated unjustly, and while he was upset about what had happened, he did not let his bitterness stand in the way of moving forward with his life. We cannot turn back time, we can only move forward and look to the past for lessons to be learned. There is a reason for everything, and lessons to be learned about every situation. Keagan knows that there will still be struggles and disappointments in his life, especially having the stigma of incarceration on his history.

People want to believe in liberty and justice for all, and for the most part, there is justice. Still, when there is injustice for one person, it is still unfair. Justice is not a one-size-fits-all solution; the way it is applied makes a big difference. I told Keagan to never let others discourage him about his past, and with determination and hard work he would succeed. When you allow anger to take over, you lose opportunities for happiness that you'll never get back. Encouragement is one of the greatest things you can give to somebody. I continue to remind Keagan that those who loved him will always be there for him. If you keep hope and faith close to your heart, you will always succeed. The past is always in the past, and the future is all we can do anything about. Don't be a prisoner of the past, but learn to live each day one day at time. Keagan's religious beliefs that he learned from a young age have helped him through the tough times in his life. No matter what your situation is, God alone knows your future, and He will not put you through any more than you can bear. If you get to it, He will get you through it.

In many cases when a crime has been committed, and the evidence proves such, those that committed the crime are given only a minor punishment. In other situations where a minor crime has been committed, these persons are given a much longer or more serious punishment. While this may seem unfair, we accept this as part of life. I believe that Keagan has accepted this as well; he knows how unjustly he was treated, but yet has a great attitude as he continues to work hard and direct his energy towards positive ventures.

Over the last few years, many persons have been finally released from prison after years of proclaiming their innocence. Yet, no one listened or took steps to investigate the facts. In many cases, it seems that the prosecutors fight more for advancing their position than for justice. Often an innocent person pays for these mistakes with part or all of their lives. When prosecuting is the focus, without any thought for the evidence, isn't there something wrong with the system? I thank God for the help I received from many organizations and persons of authority to help my son eventually find justice.

Recently a man was released after twenty years of punishment, and a wasted life for something that he did not do. Many others have also been released after the evidence finally proves them innocent. They have to start their lives over years later. In the case of a Central Park rapist, the so-called criminal was proven innocent after serving a number of years in prison. Every time I hear of such injustice, my heart sinks, and I pray that God will grant these people strength to move forward in a positive manner.

Isn't it ironic that when a person has been proven innocent for a crime they did not commit, there still seems to be much hesitation for the system to willingly free the innocent person? In my son's case, there was reluctance to admit the mistake, and compensation was never granted. A mere apology will never give the wasted years of a person's life back. Someone should be held responsible for the wrong that the person has suffered, especially when facts and evidences are concealed and/or ignored by the justice system.

CHAPTER NINE
HANDICAP JUSTICE

Another injustice that breaks my heart is the treatment of some of our soldiers. My oldest brother Jessie served in the Vietnam War, and my Uncle Walter served in World War II. They were sent off to fight for our freedom, and forced to face many difficulties, inadequate equipment, and horror of many kinds. When some of our soldiers returned home, some were treated as strangers or even criminals. Some of these men served two terms in the war, but when they returned home and requested citizenship, it was slow to be granted or completely denied. They were good enough to fight for the United States, but not enough to become a citizen. I find this very disturbing. Ironically, it seems that these soldiers defended their right to be disrespected. Some returned home with various injuries, both physical and emotional, but were given little treatment, if any. These veterans were told that they could not receive treatment because the proper paperwork was missing or some other excuse. Isn't it amazing how the paperwork was available when it was time for those persons to go off to the war? Often, when a soldier has been severely injured and not able to pursue employment, no proper compensation is given them to support themselves or their families. I find it amazing how the government funds the war, but not the casualties of the war.

I was listening to a soldier on the news one afternoon, and he stated that he had received documents that instructed him to pay for some equipment that was either damaged or destroyed. This was something that had supposedly occurred ten years prior, and the commander in charge at the time had since passed away. Such a situation seemed so unfair.

I find it amazing that our government seems to focus and spend money on certain things, but somehow miss the real target. One great example is that our government has wasted millions of dollars on ice that was purchased and later destroyed in connection with Hurricane Katrina. One would think that maybe that money could have been designated to for better living facilities, instead of the toxic trailers provided to the poor victims of the hurricane. Maybe you wonder why the levee wasn't constructed properly, for it was known that the levee was not built properly to be strong enough to hold back the force of the water. Perhaps this levee might have been corrected had it been used in a richer community.

The winds of Hurricane Katrina blew open the covers of a lot of prejudices and biases. I can't help but wonder why it took our government so long to respond to the emergency, as hundreds of people were drowning or lay dying of heat exhaustion. There was no food, no drinking water, and no bathroom facilities. These people were basically trying to survive in hell. The United States is one of the riches countries in the world, and our citizens were left in this situation for weeks before help arrived. Even after help arrived for these poor victims, the trailers given them contained toxins that caused illness to the occupants. Several years have passed, and still many people have not been able to return to their homes. In many neighborhoods very little work if any has been done to restore them. The citizens feel that they are invisible, with incompetent leadership. The insurance companies have used arguments of flood or hurricane damage in order to not have to pay claims that these people need in order to begin rebuilding their homes and begin their lives once again.

Treatment for both physical and mental conditions are lacking. The government is doling out millions of dollars to large corporations for construction, while minority contractors seem to be overlooked for employment. Frustration, depression, and stress disorders are increasing; crime rates are going up, and suicides are increasing. Where is the justice? Let's see what develops in the devastated area of the Katrina hurricane in the next few years. Perhaps a major cooperation will happen to purchase the land with the help of governmental assistance. Most likely, levees will be constructed to withhold the water properly. Then these properties will most likely be sold or leased for thousands to even millions of dollars. The poor people that originally owned the property will be long gone, because the insurance companies denied these people even the basic assistance owed them. Unfortunately, we accept this as normal. Our country is one of the wealthiest countries in the world, and yet we have thousands of hungry and homeless people living in substandard conditions. Just think about how this could be you or me the next time around.

And yet our government was pursuing this poor solider for restitution of equipment; he had risked his life for defending our country. Where is the justice in that? Such unfairness and injustice needs to corrected whenever it is encountered. If this soldier had deliberately damaged government property, it would be understandable to ask for restitution, but not when it was only being used in the manner it was intended. Wouldn't the world be much better if when a mistake was made, we immediately took steps to correct it, instead of looking for excuses? All people should be willing to admit when a mistake is made, as everyone makes mistakes. No one is perfect, only God is perfect.

There are many men and women that have worked very hard to protect our country and did everything that was asked of them, completing their original commitment, only to be told that their tour of duty has been extended. Most likely these men and women were disappointed and upset, as they were looking forward to completing their commitment, and returning home to their families and friends. Is this fair? The number of soldiers and military personnel that commit suicide has increased. Is this suicide rate increasing because of the diminishing care and concern for the soldiers that are risking their lives for our freedom?

In the wake of the horrible tragedy of September 11, 2001, firemen, policemen and other workers worked diligently for months, and many became ill after inhaling the toxins there. Still many of these people were denied basic medical treatment and compensation. Where is the justice?

Have you ever stop to think there is something wrong with the social security system? Older citizens often have to decide whether to purchase expensive medication that they need, or food and other necessities, as they cannot afford both. Yet, there is no increase in social security benefits for persons in such a predicament. Congress has very little interest, if any, in social security, because they get a salary for life, not social security. Where is the justice? I wonder why many medications and foods are still being distributed to thousands of people, when they have been proven to cause harmful side effects, and sometimes even death. Many of these studies were done years before these products ever hit the shelves, but the information was kept secret. What is wrong with this? Where is the justice?

How can we spend billions of dollars to experiment on Mars, the Moon and outer space, looking for signs of life, but ignore about six billion signs of life in our own planet. Many are homeless, sick, and experiencing devastation, desperation and heartbreak, but we do not use the resources to assist in these known crises. Science and technology are very important, and America should be number one in these challenges. Maybe it is time that we reexamine our priorities. It doesn't seem that we have our priorities in order when we can find billions of funding for different projects, but neglect human suffering that is prevalent around our planet.

There are many families that have experienced nightmares with loved ones that are serving in different wars. My nephew served twenty-five years, with some of that time being in Iraq. Even though he had served his time, and was ready for retirement, the army was reluctant to process the paper work to allow him to do so. He was told that if he retired at that time, he would receive one hundred dollars less per month in his retirement. I immediately began praying after I heard this, and urged him to pray also. He had worked hard, and achieved his Master's Degree in Business, that should be able to get him a job. My friends and family laughed at me when I told him that even if he did not find a job right away, he could pick up aluminum cans. They continued to laugh, and asked if I lost my mind. I told them no; it would be an honest thing to do. The main thing is that he would be home finally. My nephew is finally home, and all thanks to God. He is basically in good health, even though he does have a minor medical condition. He is still blessed and pursuing employment.

CHAPTER TEN

THE OTHER WOMAN'S DRAMA

In spite of everything, life continues on. The relationship between Ethan and my next-door neighbor, who I'll call Donna, continued between New York and North Carolina. She would visit him, and when he came back to New York, he would visit with her. One day, Donna decided to visit Ethan in North Carolina unannounced. When she arrived in North Carolina, she found Ethan sitting in his car with another girlfriend. Needless to say, Donna was very upset, and she approached the car to have words with this woman. She told the woman that Ethan was her man for over twelve years. She also told her that Ethan had cheated on his wife, cheated on her, and most likely would cheat on this new girlfriend as well. Donna did some damage to the car, and the police were called.

After this, everyone in the small town knew about the affair and the events that had taken place. Donna talked her situation over with a friend, and discussed the lengthy relationship that she and Ethan had shared. She said she could not believe that he could do that to her. You can tell whatever you want to whoever you want, but the truth always has a way of somehow coming out.

After Ethan's car was damaged, there was more legal drama in progress for Ethan and Donna. Donna had testified in the North Carolina court that she had been in a relationship with him for over twelve years, and it was found that both had lied under oath in the New York court when they stated that they only had only a business relationship.

After the conclusion of the court session in North Carolina, there was additional drama between Donna and Ethan. They had a heated argument about the New York court testimony, and Donna ended up physically assaulting Ethan. She was then escorted out of the courthouse by the court officers. It has been said, "Birds of a feather flock together." You will associate and spend the majority of your time with the people of which you are the most comfortable. If a person spends a lot of time with people of questionable character, they must have something in common. Our choices determine our destiny, and every choice has consequences.

Don't waste precious energy and time on people that will only bring you down. If you spend time with such people, you will eventually be brought down to their level. Focus your time and energy on improving your life. Use past experiences to improve your future. Don't let past failures deter you or rob you of happiness. Excuses are the most crippling disease, and failure is the prognosis. Keep in mind your goals; great love and achievement involve much risk. Create goals, and cultivate a burning desire to achieve them.

Ethan told Keagan about the court date that he had in New York regarding Donna's situation. He asked Keagan, "Does your mother know about the court drama with Donna?" Keagan answered, "Yes." After Ethan had lied to me all these years, it must have been hard for the truth to come out. The court date was approaching, and Ethan asked Keagan to come to court with him. Keagan told Ethan that he created the situation for himself, and asked him if his cheating was worth it. Ethan needed to take responsibility for his choices.

Keagan explained to Ethan that since he was self-employed, he only got paid when he worked. Ethan had never offered Keagan any assistance after he was released from prison. I was glad that our son had discussed this matter with his father, and let him know he could no longer fool people any longer. Keagan told me about this conversation later, and I told him that he was a grown man, and could make his own decisions. I advised him not to put himself in a situation that was more negative than positive, if he could avoid it. Ethan was only looking out for himself.

The court date arrived, and Ethan came back to New York, and stayed with his cousin Monica. He attended court that day, and when Ethan didn't return back to the apartment later that evening, Monica called Keagan inquiring about his whereabouts. Keagan told me about the conversation. Later that evening, Monica called and made some negative comments about Donna. Later, we found out that the reason that no one had heard from Ethan after court was that he had been in jail for violation of a court order of protection that Donna had issued against him. It was stated that he violated the order by making an attempt to visit her at her home; Ethan denied this ever happened. He was released, and processed for a future court appearance. During this time, Donna learned the truth behind the many lies that Ethan had told her. I am sure this was not how she expected everything would turn out. Ethan decided to take legal action against Donna for the false arrest. These court proceedings are still pending.

One would think that Ethan might have learned something from his relationship with me and with Donna, but soon after this, his new girlfriend , who I'll call Joyce, was also cheated on. It appears that Joyce had called Ethan a number of times, trying to reach him about a piece of jewelry that she had left there. After not being able to reach him by telephone, Joyce went to his residence. Since his car was parked outside, Joyce knew Ethan was home. Ethan finally answered the door, and Joyce discovered another woman inside. Of course, Joyce was very angry and disappointed, and after some heated discussion, she left.

One day, Keagan received a call from someone named Mark who claimed to be his brother. Keagan was speechless, and wanted to know if this was a joke and what was going on. After all these years of growing up an only child, he now finds out that he had a brother; a sibling. As soon as Keagan found this out, he started to ask Mark details about how they were related. Mark told Keagan that he too had never known about him all these years, and was angry and very disappointed. Keagan found out that Mark is nine months older than him, and grew up in New York, not far from where Keagan grew up. Mark attended St. John University about twenty minutes from where Keagan lived. Mark even knew Ethan's older brother, who is now deceased. Obviously a number of family members knew about Mark, but Ethan should have introduced the boys, so they could have had some type of relationship growing up.

Mark had found out about Keagan, and had also learned about and made contact with a sister, Veronica. Keagan and I had already known about Veronica. Several years previous, we had been visiting with Ethan, Mother, and other family members, and the birth of Veronica had been accidentally told. Mark arranged to meet Keagan and other family members. Ethan became upset because somehow he had thought that he could still keep this matter a secret after all this time. His sins were now too many to keep secret, and he could no longer control the situation.

Keagan asked Ethan why he had never told him about Mark, and denied them a chance to have a relationship while they were growing up. Ethan told Keagan, "If I would have told you, you would not have had a father, because your mother would have divorced me." I find it ironic that men like Ethan want to hold on their wife and home life, but yet live a lie. This type of relationship is not fair to anyone involved, especially the children. Keagan, Mark and Veronica were all disappointed and a bit angry about finding out that they had been deceived and robbed of their siblings growing up. Keagan was even more hurt because he had had no other siblings while he was growing up. These facts prove that Ethan was having an affair with Mark's mother around the same time that we were married, and maintained a relationship with her throughout the marriage. This double life accounted for some of his so-called unscheduled work time, and some of the other excuses he gave me. In many ways I felt like a single mother taking our son to karate, Little League, Cub Scouts, and other school activities. Ethan never seemed to have time to attend our son's activities and plans, even though he knew about them well in advance. Many times I would have to reschedule or cancel my plans to make sure that our son was able to attend these different functions.

Communication continued between Mark and Keagan, and they finally were able to meet. Mark had been living in Tennessee, but came to New York to visit Keagan. The boys had described what they looked like, and what they would be wearing, so they recognized each other right away. From the moment they first met, it seemed as if they had known each other much longer. Keagan was also able to meet Mark's mother.

As the news of Mark traveled throughout the family, it turned out that some of the family didn't even know that Mark existed. Keagan and I talked at length about Mark. I told him that he and Mark had now accepted each other, and that they should enjoy being brothers from now on, because one cannot turn back time. Keagan has learned over the years that wasting time pondering past mistakes, embarrassing behavior, and negative ventures is not productive. One should use the efforts and energy to build meaningful relationships. Learn whatever lessons you can from each experience; even when you lose, don't lose the lesson. No one knows how long they have on this earth, therefore it is important to make each day count towards succeeding to your goals. There are many people and things that can influence your decisions in making progress. The most important thing to do is stay focused.

A family wedding was scheduled for August, and was to be held in Maryland. Keagan and I were both invited, which generated much discussion among the family about Ethan and I, for this would be the first time that we had been in each other's company since the divorce. Perhaps they assumed there would be some type of drama between Ethan and me. We decided to attend, even though I knew it was going to be difficult seeing Ethan again. Keagan and I got up early that Saturday morning, and drove from New

York to Ft. Washington, Maryland. We arrived there early that afternoon, but Ethan and his brother were not there yet, because they had gone into town for a few hours. When Ethan and his brothers arrived, I greeted the brothers warmly, but was only cordial to Ethan. He then brought a bouquet of flowers for me, and said, "Happy Birthday." I took the flowers and said, "Thank You." Ironically, it was near my birthday, but in all the years we were together he almost never remembered my birthday, let alone did anything special.

The evening's activities began, and the bride's and groom's families became better acquainted. A number of the family members were surprised to see Keagan and I there. We exchanged greetings, and everyone was civil that evening. The nieces and nephews were very happy to see us, especially Keagan, as it had been a number of years since they had seen him. It was a reunion of sorts, and many family members became re-acquainted. The next morning, I rode with the wedding party in the limousine to the church where the wedding was to be held. As we were loading into the limousine, I noticed Ethan standing on the balcony with some other people. I couldn't help but notice the intensity in his eyes as he watched me climb into the limousine. A couple of people commented that Ethan couldn't keep his eyes off me, and I just smiled. It felt good to be flattered, but I refused to allow any kind of scene or discussion to take place. I was very aware that a number of family members expected to see some kind of drama unfold. Thankfully nothing happened.

I wanted to make sure nothing I said or did could be misinterpreted by Ethan or any of his family, therefore I tried as much as possible to avoid him and was emphatic and direct when I said "No" to basically anything Ethan asked me to do. It is important to eliminate misunderstanding whenever possible. Make sure your intentions are known by both your words and your actions. As luck would have it, I found that I had been seated at the same table with Ethan at the wedding reception. I thankfully saw the table first, and noticed that we had been seated next to each other as well. I quietly switched his name with a gentleman on the other side of the table. The evening went well, but Ethan continued to seek me out, asking me to dance or just trying to start up a conversation. I tried to avoid him as much as possible, and the evening went about as good as could be expected.

CHAPTER ELEVEN
LIFE'S LESSON 101

After the wedding, Keagan and I prepared to travel back home to New York. Everyone said their good-byes, and we had a safe trip back to New York. About a week later, I found out that one of the ladies at the wedding, Monica, had talked to some of the other guests about returning home with me, but she didn't talk to me at all. Somehow she was hurt by this, and I was made aware that she no longer wished to be friends with me. Ethan was discussing the matter with her, and she indicated to him that she was finished with me, as Ethan told Keagan. I didn't know what I could've done, because I couldn't read her mind. I usually go out of my way to assist people, so I decided that I wouldn't let the situation bother me further. There was no communication between Monica and I for approximately five months. Months later, Monica telephoned me after Keagan had visited her. Keagan explained that such small pettiness should be put aside, because life is too short for holding on to such nonsense.

After I left Verizon, I began working at the fur vault at Macy's. I tried to work hard in order to get out of the debt I had incurred during the divorce. I have worked at the fur vault for over three years, and it has proved to be very interesting. Since I had always worked in corporate management, I had no idea how I would do in retail business. Over the years, I have had some negative experiences with sales people on the telephone, and was reluctant to work in such a line of work myself. I have had many experiences with telemarketers who had no respect for my time, and since I've always been a people person, I didn't want to intrude on another person's life in such a way. One of my favorite life lessons is to treat everyone as you would like to be treated. It works with almost everyone!

After I started my job at the fur vault, my work has been a continuous life experience. I have come across very different people on a daily basis. People can be very different, but yet very much the same. They have different names, cultures and backgrounds, but the personalities and behavior are very similar as I had found in my other line of work. I had to adjust to the retail business, as it is different from my previous job as a manager in a corporate office. Each retail associate's salary is enhanced by commissions that are based on sales. There is a high level of competition, and sometimes there are disagreements to whom the sale belongs. They have a system in place to give each associate a turn to serve a customer. Some associates did not honor this system, which created problems among the other associates.

One day, I arrived at the office only to overhear a rather heated disagreement between two associates. One of the ladies believed that the other had gone into the computer, and changed the data to show that the sale belonged to her. Over the next few weeks, these ladies continued to argue over the sales, until the manager was finally able to resolve it. Our manager was very accommodating to everyone. He especially tried to work with the younger workers, as many of them were still in school. Our sales team was made up of many different cultures and religions, but we got along well for the most part. I became friends with several of the ladies in that department. In many ways, I felt like a sister to a couple of these ladies, and we would share some of our experiences with one another.

I believe strongly in the power of communication. It has worked in the past, it works in the present and it will work in the future. It is important that you make sure that you are understood, and you understand others; say what you mean and mean what you say. I wanted my fellow workers to succeed, and I developed some wonderful friendships at the fur vault. One day, two African American ladies walked into the fur salon. I greeted them as I did with all my customers, and asked if I could help them with anything. They looked at me gratefully, and then proceeded to tell me about an experience they had just had at another store. They had been looking to purchase two fur coats, but not one person greeted them or even asked if they needed help. Several associates watched them, but did nothing to assist them. The looks they were given seem to say that they should not be there, for they probably couldn't afford such finery. They had been so disgusted by the disrespect and treatment that they received that they walked out without buying anything.

These ladies bought two of our most expensive fur coats from me, and thanked me again for treating them with respect. They told me that if they wanted anything in the future, they would be back to see me. They also promised to send their friends and co-workers to see me as well. These ladies may not have looked very wealthy, but they were both executives from a major company. Pre-judging can cause both embarrassment and a loss of business. This could be a great lesson in customer service.

One would think that after a hundred years of the heartache and pain caused by racial biases, we would have learned from our mistakes and changed our behavior. Still, many incidents of prejudice and bias exist today. Swastika stickers and hanging of nooses are not just found in our history books. Many of our young people find these symbols funny, or as a way to get noticed. It is the responsibility of the adults and guardians of these young people to explain the meaning and hurt that these types of hate symbols represent. It is time for the insensitivity and the disrespectful acts to end. We still have a long way to go to truly accept each person as an equal. The human mind has been slow to change, and many prejudices and biases are so embedded that they don't even realize that they are passing them on to future generations. We must learn to see beyond color, and focus on what makes us human.

There have been other experiences at the fur vault that I have learned and grown from. Disagreements between the associates over commissions continue to occur. I try to encourage my co-workers to try to communicate with one another to resolve any issues, and move on. This is important for many aspects of the human life.

At the time of writing this book, Ethan is still living in North Carolina with a girlfriend, as I have been told. I hope that he has found some form of happiness in his life. I have heard from mutual friends and family that he regrets the divorce, and much of his behavior. I honestly wish him well, and hope that God will be with him. This chapter of my life is closed, and I no longer wish to dwell on the hurt he caused me. My life has changed in many ways, but it is now for the better.

Keagan is still working very hard, and trying to move forward with his life as he leaves his past behind him. I am still employed at Macy's fur vault, as well as being involved in my church activities and trying to assist others. I literally take one day at a time, with "One Day at a Time" being one of my favorite songs. I love to sing; I sing in the church choir and with another singing group. I have been asked to sing "One Day at a Time" at different funerals and other various programs. I am always happy to oblige. Everyone is usually very pleased and grateful. So, we just keep moving forward. We do not know what is in store for us tomorrow, and we don't know our destiny, but we can continue to move forward, one day at a time.

CHAPTER TWELVE

LOVE LIFE

Throughout this book I have talked about my relationship with God. I am sure that thousands of others can relate to God's power, regardless of what religious experience you have. Most people admit that there is a higher power somewhere in the universe that created the things that we take for granted each day. When I look at some of the beautiful scenery throughout the world, I can only be awed by the obvious touch of the Creator's hand. He created each beautiful sunset, and the beautiful sunrise. The rain is in His command. How can you not believe in God when you watch thousands of different species of animals and birds provide and care for their own? Birds and animals somehow know to migrate in the winter, and return in the spring.

I find the whole ecological system so amazing. Bees pollinate plants and flowers that are essential for both human and animal survival. They do this as they make honey for their own survival. How can you explain this if you don't believe in a God? Some animals mate for life, a perfect union in these lower species. I cannot help but wonder if much of the human race can learn from these animals. Take some quiet time to observe and appreciate the beauty of God's nature, you too can't help but realize and appreciate the omnipotent power of God.

I have learned that one must work hard and hope for the best in life. A procrastinator will never get anything done. I have learned to let the wounds of my past heal; otherwise they will continue to bleed, and I will never be able to move forward. I have learned to encourage, love, forgive and forget. A spoken word is forever free; it is impossible to take something back once it has been said. Wasted time can never been recovered, and a missed opportunity can never be returned. Now is the only time that any of us has, and we need to make the most of it. Success is not measured in money, fame or power, but in the ability to touch another person's life and leave the world a little better than when you entered it. A dying person doesn't think about all the money they have earned, or the rewards they have been given, but of the memories that they have experienced. Harboring anger, pride and unforgiveness will eventuall destroy a person. Life is full of disappointment and of success; it is a learning and growing experience. Hold tight to your ambitions and dreams. God has promised a safe landing, but He never said it would be a smooth ride.

Try to live a good life, love and respect yourself and others. Love is the fruit of the human spirit, and the most powerful force in life. A person that takes advantage of you does not truly love you. Love and treat each person as you would want to be loved and treated. Tell the truth, and be honest with yourself. Always do your best each day, and let your actions speak for you.

Someone once said that life is like a roll of toilet tissue, the closer it gets to the end of the roll, the faster it goes. Life is too short not to have fun, so make the best out of your life. Think good thoughts, learn to laugh at yourself, and count your blessings. When you get older and begin to think back on your life, you will have good memories to enjoy. One of the worst feelings in life is regret; so make choices that you can be proud of later. Don't worry about driving an expensive car, but focus on providing transportation for those who have none. Don't try to own the largest or most expensive home, but rather focus on how many people that you can welcome into your home. It is not important how many friends you have, but how many people to whom you were friendly. Those who share what God has blessed them with will be blessed with even more. Many children have been given a better opportunity from a kind heart who decided to be unselfish. Children do not understand political boundaries or borders; they just know that they are hungry, cold and homeless. There are people around us every day that need our help, all we need to do is open our eyes and ears. A single act of kindness can be a contagious spirit that can change our world. Some of the most satisfying work is helping others. You cannot help but be changed when you see the heartfelt joy and appreciation on the faces of those you helped. Even though when you are confronted with your own adversity, catastrophe and tragedy, you can help yourself most by helping others. If you look inward to your own despair, you will find yourself caving in. If you look outward to help another person, you will find you are uplifted. Show compassion to those you meet; help isn't always money; it may mean a helping hand, a listening ear, an inconvenient trip to visit somebody. If you take the time to help others, you will find that your life has been irrevocably changed for the better.

Life has its ups and downs, highs and lows; the roads are not paved, and brick walls are encountered for a reason. How you deal with life's challenges is what really matters. Give your problems over to the Lord, and He will do the rest. Keep your faith strong, it is your greatest asset. Cultivate happiness; life is much sweeter than bitter if you know where to look. Trials generate courage to keep us strong. Learn to control your emotions, and think rationally. Our sorrows remind us that we are human, and our failures keep us humble. We can do the difficult things, but God will do the impossible.

Even though some people make our lives more difficult, there are many more people that will uplift you. No matter how bad your life gets, there is ALWAYS a way through. Don't allow yourself to pull away from others; true friends can make your burdens easier and your sorrows less. The seeds you plant today will soon turn into fruit that will be harvested. Your decisions shape your life. When someone reaches out to you, don't be afraid to love them back. You never know where you will find another true friend. Practice patience and tolerance. The most beautiful attire is a smile, and it is understood by every cultural and language. Peace and love starts with a smile.

The most precious gift happens when you share love and reach out to others. The good deeds you do today may eventually benefit someone you love. Focus on making the world a better place in even a small way; after all, isn't that what life is all about?